Snowboarding

BY LAURA HAMILTON WAXMAN

AMICUS HIGH INTEREST • AMICUS INK

Amicus High Interest and Amicus Ink are imprints of Amicus
P.O. Box 1329, Mankato, MN 56002
www.amicuspublishing.us

Library of Congress Cataloging-in-Publication Data
Names: Waxman, Laura Hamilton.
Title: Snowboarding / by Laura Hamilton Waxman.
Description: Mankato, Minnesota : Amicus High Interest,
  [2018] | Series: Winter olympic sports | Includes index.
Identifiers: LCCN 2016041973 (print) | LCCN 2017006910
  (ebook) | ISBN 9781681511528 (library binding) | ISBN
  9781681521831 (pbk.) | ISBN 9781681512426 (ebook)
Subjects: LCSH: Snowboarding–Juvenile literature.
Classification: LCC GV857.S57 W38 2018 (print) | LCC
  GV857.S57 (ebook) | DDC 796.939–dc23
LC record available at https://lccn.loc.gov/2016041973

Editor: Wendy Dieker
Series Designer: Kathleen Petelinsek
Book Designer: Aubrey Harper
Photo Researcher: Holly Young

Photo Credits: ZUMA Press, Inc./Alamy Stock Photo cover;
Mike Egerton/PA Images/Alamy Stock Photo 4, 6–7; STR/
EyePress EPN/Newscom 8; AP Photo/Odd Andersen 11;
AP Photo/Sean Kilpatrick, CP 12–13; Mike Ehrmann/Getty
Images 15; Cameron Spencer/Getty Images 16; Julian Finney/
Getty Images 19; AP Photo/Luca Bruno 20; Sergey Ilnitsky/
EPA european pressphoto agency b.v./Alamy Stock Photo 23;
AP Photo/Sergei Grits 24–25; AP Photo/The Canadian Press,
Jacques Boissinot 27; Roman Vondrous/CTK/Alamy Stock
Photo 28

Printed in the United States of America

HC 10 9 8 7 6 5 4 3 2
PB 10 9 8 7 6 5 4 3

Table of Contents

Billy Morgan of Great Britain grabs his board during a trick.

Going for the Gold

A snowboarder sails into the air. The crowd cheers as he grabs his board. He spins and flips. They hoot and holler. He makes a perfect landing. The crowd goes wild. Snowboarding is an exciting mix of surfing, skateboarding, and skiing. It became a part of the Olympics in 1998. Since then, its popularity has taken off.

Some snowboarding events
are scored by judges. Other
events are races. They
depend on pure speed.
And some combine judges'
scores with racing times.
Either way, snowboarding
takes strength, skill,
and style. Only the best
snowboarders will bring
home the gold.

Sweden's Sven Thorgren
soars down the slopes
in the 2014 Olympics.

Gold medalist Jamie Anderson has been a US snowboard star since 2006.

 Why does the US beat other countries in snowboarding?

Americans like Shaun White have wowed the crowds. They do amazing moves. But the US men didn't do as well in 2014. Snowboarders from other countries have been catching up.

US women have always held the spotlight, though. One star is Jamie Anderson. She won gold in 2014. Chloe Kim is one to watch. She scored a perfect 100 in a **national event** in 2016.

 The sport was invented in the United States. US athletes have been snowboarding the longest.

Halfpipe

Swish! Twist! Flip! You might see tricks like this at the skate park. There it's called vert. But on the snow, it's called halfpipe. Snowboarders zigzag down the pipe-shaped slope of packed snow. Along the way, they go up its curved walls. At the top, they soar into the air and do tricks.

Ryo Aono of Japan does a trick above the halfpipe rim in the 2010 Olympics.

Judges score snowboarders on how well they do their tricks. They get up to 100 points for one **run** down the halfpipe. Harder tricks get more points. Creative tricks win points, too. So does getting high into the air. Snowboarders are also scored on how well they land.

Snowboarders score points on the halfpipe when they get air.

Slopestyle

Leap! A snowboarder hops onto a rail. Whoosh! He glides down it and makes a smooth landing. But he's only just begun. The slopestyle event happens on an exciting **obstacle** course. Snowboarders face rails, gaps, and **jumps**. Along the way, they do trick after trick. They need to impress the judges.

Olympic slopestyle snowboarders make riding down a rail look easy.

Australia's Torah Bright slides off an obstacle in a slopestyle run.

 When was slopestyle added to the Olympics?

The judges watch each snowboarder carefully. They pay attention to the whole run. They look extra closely at the tricks. New trick? Points. Hard trick? Even more points. Big air? Lots of points. Finally, if the judges see a smooth landing, the points go up even higher. Riders can get up to 100 points for a run.

 It became part of the Olympics in 2014. US snowboarders won gold in the men's and women's events.

Snowboard Cross

Ready, set, go! Snowboard cross is a racing event. It's also called boardercross. The race takes place on a narrow and curvy **course**. The course is filled with snowy bumps and jumps. Racers must keep up their speed while facing these obstacles. They must also stay inside the blue lines.

 Is snowboard cross dangerous?

Four snowboarders speed to the bottom of the hill in a snowboard cross race.

 Yes. Some people say it's the most dangerous Winter Olympic event. Some racers have gotten badly hurt on the course.

Racers try not to crash as they fly over a jump in the 2014 snowboard cross final.

Four to six racers race at a time. They shoot out of the starting gate. Then they speed down the course. They try to edge each other out to take the lead. But they must be careful. Racers can knock into each other and wipe out. The top racers face off in one final race for gold.

Parallel Giant Slalom

Two snowboarders zig and zig down a slope. They are racing against each other. This event is the parallel giant **slalom**. It's called that because the riders race on side-by-side courses. Each course has the same number of **gates**. Red or blue flags mark the gates. The racers must weave around their gates at top speeds.

Two snowboarders curve around their gates in a race to the finish.

Slalom racers use special snowboards for their event. The boards are longer and narrower than other boards. They are also stiffer. These boards can dig into the snow. This helps racers make sharp turns around gates. Tight snowboarding suits help, too. They cut down on **air resistance**.

Longer, narrower boards are built for speed down the slalom course.

Getting Bigger

A new event in the Olympics is big air. The snowboarder begins by zooming down a steep slope. Next comes a tall jump. The snowboarder shoots high into the air and does a trick. This is the snowboarder's chance to wow the judges. Snowboarders are scored on this one trick and the landing.

Big air has been a part of the
Snowboard World Cup for years.
It's new to the 2018 Olympics.

The 2014 snowboard cross medalists celebrate their wins on the podium. Eva Samkova (center) wears a painted mustache for luck.

The crowd goes wild for snowboarding at the Olympics. And the sport grows every year. In 1998, there were only two snowboarding events. The 2018 Winter Games are set to have five events. Where will snowboarding go in the future? How big will the tricks get? Keep your eyes on the slopes to find out!

Glossary

air resistance The slowing force on a moving object as it moves through air.

course The slope or track in a snowboarding event.

gate In slalom snowboarding, a set of poles that a snowboarder must weave around.

jump A ramp on a course that snowboarders jump over to do tricks.

national event A competition in the United States other than the Olympics; some national events are try-outs for the Olympics.

obstacle An object on the course that a snowboarder must go over, such as a jump or rail.

run In snowboarding, one time down a course.

slalom A winding race down a hill marked by gates or flags for racers to go around.

Read More

Bailer, Darice. *Snowboard Cross*. Minneapolis: Lerner Publications, 2014.

Howell, Brian. *Great Moments in Olympic Snowboarding*. Minneapolis: Abdo, 2015.

Hunter, Nick. *The Winter Olympics*. Chicago: Heinemann-Library, 2014.

Websites

Team USA
www.teamusa.org/Media/Games/Sochi-2014/Preview/ Team-USA/Snowboarding

US Snowboarding
http://ussnowboarding.com/snowboarding

Winter Olympic Events
www.timeforkids.com/news/winter-olympic- events/137746

Index

About the Author

Laura Hamilton Waxman has written and edited many nonfiction books for children. She loves learning about new things—like snowboarding—and sharing what she's learned with her readers. She lives in St. Paul, Minnesota.